THE GREATEST PRAYER

EVER PRAYED

by

J.C. McPheeters

First Fruits Press
Wilmore, Kentucky
c2012

asburyseminary.edu
800.2ASBURY
204 North Lexington Avenue
Wilmore, Kentucky 40390

First Fruits
THE ACADEMIC OPEN PRESS OF ASBURY SEMINARY

ISBN: 9781621710196

The Greatest Prayer Ever Prayed, by J.C. McPheeters.
First Fruits Press, © 2012
Pentecostal Publishing Company, [194-?]

Digital version at
http://place.asburyseminary.edu/firstfruitsheritagematerial/16/

McPheeters, J. C. (Julian Claudius), 1889-1983.
    The greatest prayer ever prayed / by J.C. McPheeters.
    Wilmore, Ky. : First Fruits Press, c2012.
    60 p. ; 21 cm.
    Reprint. Previously published: Louisville, Ky. : Herald Press, [194-?].
    ISBN: 9781621710196 (pbk.)
    1. Jesus Christ -- Prayers. 2. Bible. N.T. John XVII -- Criticism,
    interpretation, etc. 3. Prayer. I. Title.
    BV234 .M36 2012

Cover design by Haley Hill

asburyseminary.edu
800.2ASBURY
204 North Lexington Avenue
Wilmore, Kentucky 40390

First Fruits
THE ACADEMIC OPEN PRESS OF ASBURY SEMINARY

THE GREATEST PRAYER
EVER PRAYED

BY

J. C. McPHEETERS

President, Asbury Theological Seminary

and

Editor, The Pentecostal Herald

HERALD PRESS

LOUISVILLE, KY.

CONTENTS

THE GREATEST PRAYER EVER PRAYED

JOHN 17

These words spake Jesus, and lifted up his eyes to heaven, and said, Father, the hour is come; glorify thy Son, that thy Son also may glorify thee:

As thou hast given him power over all flesh, that he should give eternal life to as many as thou hast given him.

And this is life eternal, that they might know thee the only true God, and Jesus Christ, whom thou hast sent.

I have glorified thee on the earth: I have finished the work which thou gavest me to do.

And now, O Father, glorify thou me with thine own self with the glory which I had with thee before the world was.

I have manifested thy name unto the men which thou gavest me out of the world: thine they were, and thou gavest them me; and they have kept thy word.

Now they have known that all things whatsoever thou hast given me are of thee.

For I have given unto them the words which thou gavest me; and they have received them, and have known surely that I came out from thee, and they have believed that thou didst send me.

I pray for them: I pray not for the world, but

for them which thou hast given me; for they are thine.

And all mine are thine, and thine are mine; and I am glorified in them.

And now I am no more in the world, but these are in the world, and I come to thee. Holy Father, keep through thine own name those whom thou hast given me, that they may be one, as we are.

While I was with them in the world, I kept them in thy name: those that thou gavest me I have kept, and none of them is lost, but the son of perdition; that the scripture might be fulfilled.

And now come I to thee; and these things I speak in the world, that they might have my joy fulfilled in themselves.

I have given them thy word; and the world hath hated them, because they are not of the world, even as I am not of the world.

I pray not that thou shouldest take them out of the world, but that thou shouldest keep them from the evil.

They are not of the world, even as I am not of the world.

Sanctify them through thy truth: thy word is truth.

As thou hast sent me into the world, even so have I also sent them into the world.

And for their sakes I sanctify myself, that they

also might be sanctified through the truth.

Neither pray I for these alone, but for them also which shall believe on me through their word;

That they all may be one; as thou, Father, art in me, and I in thee, that they also may be one in us: that the world may believe that thou hast sent me.

And the glory which thou gavest me I have given them; that they may be one, even as we are one:

I in them, and thou in me, that they may be made perfect in one; and that the world may know that thou hast sent me, and hast loved them, as thou hast loved me.

Father, I will that they also, whom thou hast given me, be with me where I am; that they may behold my glory, which thou hast given me: for thou lovedst me before the foundation of the world.

O righteous Father, the world hath not known thee: but I have known thee, and these have known that thou hast sent me.

And I have declared unto them thy name, and will declare it; that the love wherewith thou hast loved me may be in them, and I in them.

CHAPTER I

Jesus spent much time in prayer. He withdrew from the crowds and went alone to pray. At times He would arise a great while before day in order to spend the early morning hours in prayer. At other times He would spend a whole night in prayer. Before breaking bread He prayed and gave thanks to His Father.

The prayer life of Jesus was constant. He ever lived in a spirit of prayer. He prayed his valedictory prayer at the Last Supper. He prayed His blood-drenched prayer in the Garden of Gethsemane. He prayed amid the agonies of the cross and His last word on the cross was a prayer of confidence in the committal of His Spirit into the hands of His Father.

He exhorted His disciples to pray,. He taught them the great pattern prayer. He said to them: "Men ought always to pray, and not to faint." Jesus taught His disciples that prayer is the avenue of approach to the father's bountiful storehouse where there is a sufficiency for every human need. He taught them that they were to fortify themselves against the darts of the enemy through prayer.

7

Jesus focalized His praying in behalf of His disciples. In His memorable prayer recorded in the seventeenth chapter of John He says: "I pray for them: I pray not for the world but for them which thou hast given me; for they are thine and all mine are thine and thine are mine; and I am glorified in them." (John 17:9, 10). Jesus not only prayed for His disciples of that day but He prayed for His disciples for all the years to come. In the same prayer He says: "Neither pray I for these alone, but for them also which shall believe on me through their word: that they all may be one; as thou, Father, art in me and I in thee, that they also may be one in us: that the world may believe that thou hast sent me." (John 17:20, 21). The prayer which Jesus prayed for His disciples under the shadow of the cross is likewise the prayer which He prayed for us. Jesus prayed that His disciples might be kept: "Holy Father, keep through thine own name those whom thou hast given me, that they may be one, as we are." He repeatedly prayed for the unity of His disciples, "that they may be one," even having the same unity of spirit as He had with the Father.

Jesus prayed that His disciples might have His joy. He says: "And now come I to thee; these things I speak in the world that they might have my joy fulfilled in themselves." It is the purpose

of Jesus that His disciples have the same joy which
He had. In the light of His prayer, Christians are
not to be sorrowful but ever rejoicing in the joy of
the Lord.

Jesus prayed that His disciples might remain in
the world to complete the work which the Father
had given them to do. He prays, "I pray not
that thou shouldst take them out of the world,
but that thou shouldst keep them from the evil."
Every life has a distinct mission in the world, a
definite work to be accomplished which has been
assigned by God. We glorify God as we fulfill this
God-given ambition. It is the first concern of Jesus that none of His disciples fail in the task that
has been assigned them under divine appointment.

Jesus prayed that His disciples might be sanctified. He prayed for their sanctification in these
words: "Sanctify them through thy truth: thy
word is truth." He prayed that they might be
cleansed and purified from all sin. He made provision for this cleansing and purifying of His disciples in His atoning death upon the cross. He
makes reference to this provision in His atoning
death when He says: "And for their sakes I sanctify myself, that they also might be sanctified
through the truth." In these words He speaks of
setting Himself apart to be crucified that His disciples might be crucified in a spiritual sense as in

the case of Paul who said: "I am crucified with Christ."

Jesus stated in His valedictory prayer that His disciples had been sent into the world in the same sense that He Himself had been sent by the Father. He says: "As thou hast sent me into the world, even so have I also sent them into the world." Under this commission there is no price to be regarded as too great to be paid in order to fulfill His will. Jesus laid aside all of the glory of heaven in order to come into the world and do His Father's will. As Jesus was sent to do the will of His Father so we are sent to do His will, regardless of what the cost may be.

Jesus prayed that His disciples might be made perfect, speaking these words: "I in them and thou in me that they may be made perfect in one; and that the world may know that thou hast sent me and hast loved them as thou hast loved me." The perfection which Jesus prays for in His disciples is a perfection of love. He concludes His valedictory prayer in the 17th chapter of John with these words: "That the love wherewith thou hast loved me may be in them and I in them." The Apostle John speaks of this perfection in love saying: "Herein is our love made perfect, that we may have boldness in the day of judgment: because as he is so are we in this world." (I John 4:17).

Jesus prayed that His disciples might finally dwell with Him where they will forever behold His glory. In His prayer in this regard we have the most comforting words of assurance and hope within the whole scope of divine revelation. Thus He prays: "Father, I will that they also, whom thou hast given me, be with me where I am; that they may behold my glory, which thou hast given me; for thou lovedst me before the foundation of the world." If we fulfill the purpose of His will in this world, we shall forever behold His glory in the world to come.

CHAPTER II

The greatest prayer ever prayed is recorded in the 17th chapter of John. This is our Lord's valedictory prayer which He prayed shortly before going to the Garden of Gethsemane and then to the cross. In the introduction of this remarkable prayer, we have the words: "Father. the hour is come." It was a momentous hour in the life of our Lord. It was an hour of supreme destiny. The index finger of prophecy across many centuries had pointed to this hour.

Gethsemane and Golgotha were just ahead. Both the tragedy and the triumph of the cross were near at hand. Jesus came to this supreme hour with confidence and assurance. No note of defeat is sounded and no expressions of cowardice are manifested as the shadows of the cross fall across His pathway.

As God had been glorified in the life of Jesus, so Jesus now expects God to be glorified in His death. Under the shadow of the cross, He prays: "Glorify thy son, that thy son also may glorify thee."

Jesus could glorify the Father in death because He had glorified the Father in life. Jesus came into the world and lived among men. He was tempted in all points like as we are. He tasted of the limitations of humanity. He knew the sting of fatigue and weariness. He knew the disappointment in the betrayal of friends. He knew the joys of the wedding feast and He knew the sorrows of the funeral procession. It was in this world with all of its disappointments, its heartaches and its reverses that Jesus glorified the Father.

Because Jesus glorified the Father in life, He has made it possible for us to glorify the Father in this world.

We may become samples of the gospel of Christ. Paul in his first epistle to the Thessalonians speaks of the fact that the Thessalonian Christians had become good examples of the saving grace of Christ. Paul says: "So that ye were ensamples to all that believed in Macedonia and Achaia."

A good example of the saving grace of God, lived in daily life, will do more to draw men to Christ than many sermons. The greatest sermon is the sermon of a life.

The sermon of a life never dies. Death cannot destroy such a sermon. The far-reaching influence of a holy life is described in these words of the Scripture: "He being dead, yet speaketh."

Two brothers who had grown to manhood, who

came from a Christian home, had failed to follow the Christ of their Godly parents. They traveled the ways of the world. After the passing of the years, there came a day when the two brothers were tearing down the old home of their childhood, to replace it with a modern building. When these brothers came to tear up the floor about the old hearthstone, one of them stopped and said to the other, "Bill, you know what we are about to do? We are about to tear up the floor about this hearthstone where father conducted family prayer. It was here that we knelt in childhood in prayer with father and mother. But we have not followed the Christ that they served."

These words were sufficient to bring both of the brothers under conviction. As they meditated and thought of the lives that had been lived before them in their parents, it turned the tide in their sinful lives. After many years had passed, through the influence of Christian parents, these brothers returned as prodigals from the far country to the Father's house.

Jesus had glorified the Father in life and the hour had now come, as is indicated in the introduction of His prayer, for Him to glorify the Father in His death. The sacrificial bleating lambs and bullocks offered upon the tabernacle and temple altars for centuries, pointed to the day when the

Lamb of God would be slain for the sins of the whole world. In that hour of unprecedented sacrifice, Christ's one purpose was to glorify the Father, and He prayed: "Now, O Father, glorify thou me with thine own self, with the glory which I had with thee before the world was."

The prayer of Jesus was answered and the Father was glorified in the Son through his atoning death upon the cross. Jesus never failed in the fulfillment of the divine purpose for human redemption. "Nevertheless, not my will, but thine be done" was the prayer of Jesus in the great hour of testing in the Garden of Gethsemane.

Jesus went immediately to the cross, because it was the will of the Father that He should taste death for every man. He faced His death without resentment or bitterness. He prayed for those who crucified Him. His last words upon the cross were words of confidence and assurance: "Father, into thy hands I commend my spirit."

When Jesus glorified the Father in death, He made it possible for His disciples likewise to glorify the Father in death. From the purely human viewpoint death is the arch-enemy of the race. But when Jesus glorified the Father in death and tasted death for every man, He made a way of victory and triumph over the very sting of death so that men may shout in triumph over this arch-enemy,

"Death where is thy sting, O grave where is thy victory?"

Many are the remarkable examples of those who have glorified God in death. John Wesley's last words were, before leaving the scene of his earthly labors: "The best of all God is with us." When Dwight L. Moody came to the crossing of the river, his last words were: "Earth is receding, heaven is opening, God is calling for me." A young ministerial student in Asbury College was stricken with a grave physical malady. His name was Dick Eddy from Oakland, Calif. The very best in medical skill was unable to check the devouring disease that preyed upon his body. Many prayers went up in his behalf, but it seemed otherwise in divine providence that he should not be a minister in this world, but that a larger ministry awaited him in another land. Dick Eddy came to the crossing of the bar on New Year's day, 1950. Shortly before he bid earth adieu, he said to his mother who was watching at his bedside: "Mother, do you hear the music?" His mother replied, "No, I don't hear the music, Dick." Then he said: "Oh, mother, surely you hear the music. It is wonderful. The music is wonderful." So Dick Eddy, a young ministerial student slipped away from earth amid music played upon the harps of gold by cherubims and seraphims.

One of the great missionary statesmen, prophets, and evangelists of our generation, at the time of the writing of this booklet stood at the gate of heaven in the evening time of life at the ripe age of fourscore and seven years. For several months he has been bedfast. He lives in Berkeley, Calif. A few months ago I stood at his bedside and said to him, as we were parting: "Dr. Wainwright, I hope you will soon be up again," and it was then that he pointed his hands feebly upward and said: "Whether up or down, it is up for me."

The world pronounced that which transpired upon the cross as ignominious defeat. The first two days following the crucifixion belonged to the world. The enemies of Jesus were satisfied that they had done away with Him. They spoke the language of the world as they glorified in the defeat of Jesus. The world heard them gladly as they proclaimed the end of the kingdom which Jesus proposed to establish.

During the first two days following the crucifixion, the words of the Apostle John were fulfilled in the discussions of men concerning the death of Jesus: "They are of the world; therefore speak they of the world and the world heareth them."

The world spoke the language of defeat while Jesus lay in the tomb. But the world does not

speak the last word. God speaks the last word.
The world has its days of seeming triumphs and
victories. Those victories are not as enduring as
they may appear. The final day is God's day. The
third day following the crucifixion of Jesus was
God's day. God's day put to shame the triumphs
and the victories of the two days that had belonged
to the world. On the third day there came again
the fulfillment of the words of the apostle. "The
world passeth away, and the lust thereof: but he
that doeth the will of God abideth forever."

The grave could not conquer Jesus, because He
had done the will of His Father. As the grave
could not conquer Jesus, the grave cannot conquer
His disciples. Every settlement and every community in all the world has its burying ground.
You may find a settlement or a community without
a bank, without a post office, without a railway station, or without a department store, but you will
find no community on the face of the earth without
a burying ground. But these burying grounds are
not the last chapter. The last word has not been
written upon marbles of stone. The last chapter
will be written when the graves shall give forth
their dead, and the mortal bodies shall put on
immortality.

The last word that is to be spoken by God in
connection with all of the burying places of the

world for His children, is described by the Apostle
Paul in the 4th chapter of 1st Thessalonians: "But
I would not have you to be ignorant, brethren, concerning them which are asleep, that ye sorrow not,
even as others which have no hope. For if we believe that Jesus died and rose again, even so them
also which sleep in Jesus will God bring with
him. For this we say unto you by the word of
the Lord, that we which are alive and remain unto
the coming of the Lord shall not prevent them
which are asleep. For the Lord himself shall de-
scend from heaven with a shout, with the voice of
the archangel, and with the trump of God: and the
dead in Christ shall rise first: Then we which are
alive and remain shall be caught up together with
them in the clouds to meet the Lord in the air: and
so shall we ever be with the Lord. Wherefore
comfort one another with these words."

The language of defeat which we hear in the
world is not to be taken at its face value, because
God always has another day, and God's day is a
day of triumph and of victory. The world had its
day with the Caesars, who ruled over Rome, the
mightiest empire ever built upon the face of the
earth. For a period of 300 years the Caesars were
arrayed against the Christian church. They
initiated the terrible persecutions of dungeon, fire
and sword, in which the lives of millions of Chris-

tians were sacrificed. Those persecutions were waged with such furor that at one time the insignia was stamped upon the Roman coin: "The Christians are no more." But the Caesars did not speak the last word.

The church of Christ is still marching in triumph over the earth. Mussolini, Hitler, and the Japanese militarists thought that they were speaking the last word concerning the new day of triumph for their regimes. But all of these regimes have gone down and are no more. At the present hour another colossal enemy to Christianity is upon the arena waging a mighty conflict. Atheistic communism is boasting of world conquest and of world victory, but atheistic communism will not have the last word. God will speak the last word himself.

We hear much concerning the great apostasy in the church and the defeat that has come to the modern church. It is true that we live in an age of apostasy, when many have turned from the true faith, but there still remains a church within the church, including all of those in all the churches who have not bowed the knee to the Baal of compromising unbelief and skepticism. This church within the church is today a mighty, invincible, conquering force that is in the world, marching on in triumph and victory from glory to glory. The

greatest spiritual conquests of the ages are trans-
piring upon the earth today. If denominations
fail, if they apostasize, if they dry up with eccles-
iastical ritualism and cold formalism, God will
still raise up a people that will carry on His work
in the world.

We are repeatedly confronted with great hours
of destiny as individuals and as nations. We are
now confronted with the great hour of destiny in
the life of the world. Old dynasties and old regimes and systems have been broken up. New
ideologies have arisen with visions of world conquest. The race of destiny is on between these
ideologies and the Christian faith.

The Macedonian call for the gospel of Christ is
coming from more people and lands, with greater
urgency than ever, in the history of the world.
From the north, the south, the east, and the west,
there comes the ancient call upon every tide of the
sea and on every breath of every wind that blows,
"Come over and help us!"

The events of recent years have reinforced
anew a call that was sent out by John R. Mott,
the great missionary statesman, something like a
generation ago. John R. Mott sent a call from
the Orient to the United States: "Send a thous-
sand missionaries to Japan now, or send a million
soldiers later." We did not send the missionaries

in anything like the number in the appeal of this missionary statesman. But we later sent more than a million soldiers. We sent four million soldiers into the terrible holocaust of the Pacific during World War II.

And God now is issuing a new challenge to the Christians of the whole world. The significance of this challenge is enforced by the words of Gen. Douglas MacArthur, who says: "We have had our last chance." God's challenge is now to evangelize the world. The only remaining hope that is upon the horizon for world security is the gospel of Jesus Christ. And God is saying to the Christians of the world today: "You must now evangelize or perish."

What we do, we must do quickly. Truly, the hour is at hand. The hour is at hand for the evangelization of the world. The hour is at hand for a nation-wide and world-wide Holy Ghost revival. The hour is at hand for heeding the voice of the Holy Spirit in a world crusade of evangelism. The hour calls for the concentration of our efforts upon the simple, fundamental saving truths of the gospel for the salvation of a lost world. It is not more organization or form, ritual or ceremony in our worship that we need. These things may prove to be only a stone in answer to the cry of the hungry multitudes for bread.

The masses are hungry for the bread of life. It is not ethics, a philosophy, or a political system that men's hearts cry for in their deepest need. The deeper cry in the souls of men is for a liberation from their inner bondage and for an inner peace that the world cannot give.

The liberation and peace for which men cry in their hearts can come only through Jesus Christ. John spoke of the abiding life of peace and victory for which men crave, in these words: "This is the record, that God has given to us, eternal life, and this life is in his Son."

The apostle also speaks of this life as one of victory which overcomes the world: "For whatsoever is born of God overcometh the world: and this is the victory that overcometh the world, even our faith."

This is a defeated world and the defeat that is in the world has come through dependence only upon human wisdom and human strength. The pagan lands that sit in darkness are defeated lands. Robert Chung is one of the great evangelists of Korea. While in this country on a furlough, I heard him tell of the great mass meetings held in that land where the people gathered by the thousands to hear the gospel. The altar services were so large that it became necessary to erect a loud speaker system and to give the penitents instructions over the loud speaker as they fell upon the ground with penitential tears seeking to know the Christ whom the evangelist preached. Robert Chung says that he has seen hundreds and hundreds of the Koreans rise from their knees with a shine upon their faces and beating their breasts with their hands, shouting aloud: "I have found Him. I have found Him." They had found the Christ, the only one who can give victory to those who sit in darkness.

Civilization stands at such an hour of destiny as has never been confronted before in human history. Men had scarcely recovered from the shock of the possibilities of the destructive power of the atomic bomb, when the announcement came from the scientific laboratories that the hydrogen bomb, a thousand times more destructive than the atomic bomb, was a potential weapon for the future. Such an eminent scientist as Einstein has warned the world that the hydrogen bomb might be developed to the point where its destructive power could destroy all life upon the planet. Civilization with her vast inventive resources is confronted with a tragic dilemma as to what these resources may mean for her future.

The hour which confronts us calls for the greatest spiritual crusade of the ages. All of the devices and inventions of modern man have failed to meet the inner cry of the hearts of men for soul rest and peace. Only Christ can calm the tempest which breaks with fury over the lonely, discouraged and despairing hearts of men. It is high time for men everywhere to concentrate upon the one supreme need of the world, Christ and Him crucified, risen again, now interceding for man at the right hand of the Father, and who is coming again in glorious majesty and power.

Anything less than a great spiritual revival will not relieve the baffling tensions between employers and employees. It is only in the wake of such a revival that political expediency for the sake of vote-getting, even at the peril of the nation, can be changed to a statesmanship which places the welfare of the nation above a mess of pottage for a political job. It is only in such a revival that we can hope again to bring God and moral restraint into our system of Godless education that is fast hurtling us on the downward road to destruction.

"The hour is come" for the renewed proclamation of the glorious gospel of Christ in the power of the Holy Ghost through the wide-open doors that now girdle the entire globe. The Macedonian call for help from the distressed peoples of the earth must be answered now or never, if their spiritual and moral needs are to be met. These urgent calls may be much shorter than we realize. The time is fast running out. What we do, we must do quickly.

CHAPTER III

The earth has been the great battleground of the ages between God and Satan and between the kingdom of light and the kingdom of darkness. When the curtain of sacred history is lifted in the first chapter of Genesis, we have revealed the scene of a contest in the Garden of Eden in which Satan bears the palm of triumph amid the tragedy of the fall of man.

God did not beat a retreat in the face of the colossal tragedy which had wrested his prize creation from His domain. God did not withdraw and leave the world in the hands of Satan, the arch enemy of all good and the grand potentate of all evil.

The redemptive stream of salvation which was eventually to flow to the peoples of every kindred and tongue, found its fountain source in the love of God amid the terrible tragedies involved in the fall of man. The divine drama of human redemption must be enacted upon earth. It was on earth that man encountered the tempter; it was on earth that man went down in the terrible wreckage and ruin of seemingly hopeless defeat. The defeat of God on earth, which the kingdoms of darkness claimed, must be retrieved upon earth if the name

26

of God is to hold preeminence over every name in heaven and in earth.

The moral conflict in the world has been intensified by the blight of the thorn which penetrates the whole of nature as the result of the fall of man. The spiritual and moral victories of life cannot be won amid the sweet aroma of a rose-scented garden but they must be won amid the thorns and thistles of severe conflict.

God sent His Son into a battle-scarred, sin-blighted world, deluged with wreckage, despair, and ruin. This act of infinite love is described by the Apostle John: "In this was manifested the love of God toward us, because that God sent his only begotten Son into the world, that we might live through him. Herein is love, not that we loved God, but that he loved us, and sent his Son to be the propitiation for our sins." (I John 4:9, 10).

In a world unfriendly to divine grace, Jesus triumphed and prevailed against the enemy. Jesus spoke of His triumph in the world in the prayer which He prayed with His disciples on the night of His betrayal. He said: "I have glorified thee on the earth; I have finished the work which thou gavest me to do." (John 17:4). Jesus had formerly glorified God in heaven amid the unending diadems and praises of all the heavenly hosts. Jesus likewise glorified the Father on earth where all the setting and environment was just the opposite of that in heaven.

Christ through His life and atoning death has likewise made it possible for all of His disciples to glorify the Father in the earth. This earth is a battleground where the eternal destinies of men are settled forever. It is here that we build for eternity, either for weal or for woe.

It is according to the will of God that His children should remain in the world for a time, that they may glorify His name in the earth. Jesus did not pray that His disciples might be taken out of the world but He prayed that they might remain in the world for a time. This is His prayer for them in this regard: "I pray not that thou shouldst take them out of the world, but that thou shouldst keep them from the evil." It is possible through the grace of God to be kept from evil in an evil world. Through Christ, it is possible to overcome the world while living in the world. The Apostle John in his first epistle says: "Ye are of God, little children, and have overcome them: because greater is he that is in you than he that is in the world." (I John 4:4).

The triumph and the victories of the Christian life are available in this world. We do not need to wait until the hour of death for complete deliverance from sin. This deliverance may be obtained through Christ while we live in the world. The Apostle John points out this glorious deliverance in these words: "But if we walk in the light as he is in the light, we have fellowship one with another and the blood of Jesus Christ his Son cleanseth us from all sin,   If we confess our sins he is faithful and just to forgive us our sins and to cleanse us from all unrighteousness." (I John 1:7, 9).

John also states that those who claim they do not need any such deliverance from sin in this life deceive themselves and the truth is not in them. He says, "If we say that we have no sin, we deceive ourselves and the truth is not in us." (I John 1:8). Many are the battles, the testings, the temptations, and disappointments as we wage the Christian warfare in this world. It is in this battle-ground of destiny that Christ Himself waged His warfare against the wicked one. It was in this world that He was "tempted in all points like as we are, yet without sin." In this world He endured the cross and suffered the shame. He was despised and rejected of men. But amid all the fury of the attacks of the wicked one, He glorified the Father on the earth.

Jesus has made available the victories which He obtained upon the earth for His disciples. We are sent into the world to glorify the Father even as Jesus was sent into the world. Jesus said of

His disciples: "As thou hast sent me into the world, even so have I also sent them into the world." (John 17:18). He not only sends us as He was sent, but He promises to give us His glory and strength to sustain us amid all of life's conflicts. He says: "And the glory which thou gavest me I have given them."

CHAPTER IV

THE MANIFESTED CHRIST

Christ was manifested in the world as the revelation of the Father. This fact is revealed in a statement of Jesus in His prayer in which He says: "I have manifested thy name unto the men which thou gavest me out of the world." (John 17:6).

John speaks of the manifested Christ in His first epistle, saying: "For the life was manifested, and we have seen it, and bear witness, and show unto you that eternal light, which was with the Father, and was manifested unto us." (I John 1:2).

Christ was manifested to the world in the manner of His birth. Christ's coming into the world was a miraculous event. The incarnation is a profound mystery, but a glorious fact. Christ's birth was different from any other ever born into the world. In the ordinary birth a new personality is created, a new being begins. The ordinary birth marks the beginning of a new life that never existed before.

But the situation was entirely different with the coming of Jesus into the world. Jesus existed before the foundation of the world. Jesus speaks of His pre-existence in His prayer in which He says: "Now, O Father, glorify thou me with thine own self with the glory which I had with thee before the world was." Jesus had no natural earthly father. This would not have been possible because Jesus already existed.

Christ's advent into the world was an incarnation. He who had existed from all eternity came clothed in human flesh. The event of His incarnation took place in the womb of a virgin through the miracle of the Holy Ghost.

The Scriptures clearly confirm His virgin birth. The prophet Isaiah foretold His birth of a virgin. The prophet said: "Therefore the Lord himself shall give you a sign; behold, a virgin shall conceive and bear a son, and shall call his name Immanuel." (Isa. 7:14).

In the first chapter of Matthew we find the genealogy of Jesus traced from Abraham to Joseph. The genealogy begins with the statement: "Abraham begat Isaac; and Isaac begat Jacob; and Jacob begat Judah and his brethren." The description of the genealogy continued in this same manner for 38 generations, but the description takes a decided change when the inspired writer comes to the generation of Joseph. If the description had continued as given for 38 generations, the passage concerning Joseph would read: "And Jacob begat Joseph and Joseph begat Jesus," but the passage does not read in any such manner. It reads thus: "And Jacob begat Joseph, the husband of Mary, of whom was born Jesus, who is called the Christ."

The miraculous elements involved in connection with Christ's coming in Bethlehem are still manifest in His continuous coming into the hearts of men throughout all ages. It is a mistake for us to make Christ's coming in Bethlehem, an historical retrospect, and think of His birth as an isolated event of history belonging to the past, which we commemorate in an annual Christmas celebration. The birth of Jesus in Bethlehem was an historical event. It was such a significant historical event that it became the dividing line of human history. But it was more than an historical event in that it has become a living event in the lives of men and women. We can only know something of the glory of Christ's coming in Bethlehem when we know the glory of His coming in our individual lives.

We have a multitude of testimonies of Christ's miraculous coming into the hearts and lives of men. These testimonies are multiplied with each passing year. Sinful and wicked men have found Him to be the only hope for deliverance from the bondage of sin. Many have turned to Him in desperation to find that He was able to give them the deliverance and the peace that their hearts craved. Only Christ has the power to be born into the hearts of men and transform human lives.

The world has been amazed at the transformation that has come to many lives when Christ was born in the heart, in a new birth of the soul. One of the more recent of these transformations took place in the city of Indianapolis in the life of a prominent florist in that city. This man was given to drink and other sinful vices. He was spending approximately $5,000 per year on liquor for himself and his friends. A very strange and unusual thing happened one night while he was dining in a restaurant. He dropped a nickel in a music box expecting some popular tune of the world, when to his utter amazement one of the great old hymns of the church began to play like "Amazing Grace." He ridiculed the song in the presence of his friends and made all manner of fun and jest at it. But when he went to his home that night, he found that he could not shake off the words and the tune of that old song. He tossed on his bed. His old sinful life stood out before him. The Spirit of God smote him with deep conviction and his heart began to cry out for deliverance from his sins. That old gospel song resulted in his conversion. He became a transformed man.

This man was the treasurer of the post of the American Legion which at that time was putting a bar into the club house of the post. He refused to write the checks to pay the bills for that bar. He told the officers of the post that he would not pay any bills or turn over the treasurer's book until he could say something to them. A meeting was called. This man came to the club house with a Bible under his arm. It was a large pulpit Bible. He walked in and placed his Bible on the bar, and then turned to the men and told them what Christ meant to him, and how his life had been changed. His testimony made a profound impression upon his comrades. Some of them were deeply moved.

I heard of this man as he was flying to different points of the country giving his testimony, paying his own expenses. I invited him to come to Asbury Theological Seminary for a chapel talk. The morning that he gave his talk, he walked down the aisle with the same pulpit Bible under his arm. He loves the Word of God and carries this Bible about as a testimony. Such procedure might sound a bit fanatical, but those who heard him realized that he was not a fanatic, but that something tremendous had happened in his life.

Christ was manifested in the life that He lived. He lived a life that no one else ever lived. He "was in all points tempted like as we are, yet without sin." Jesus lived in the world, but was not of the world. No situation in life overwhelmed

Him. He was as unfrustrated in the presence of the storm as amid the calmness of a June morning. He prayed for those who despitefully used Him. No one ever entrapped Him in conversation in their efforts to outwit Him. Even at the early age of twelve years, His wisdom was more than a match for the wise men in the temple.

The life of Jesus was not lived on the low plane of the sordid, the sensual and the selfish. He lived and moved in the high altitudes of infinite love. He manifested a love for all men, even for His enemies. In His dying moments upon the cross, He prayed for those who crucified Him.

The life of Jesus towers in sublime grandeur over all events and all lives of all ages, like a mighty snow-capped peak towering high above all other peaks in a far-flung range of mountains. Such a peak may manifest itself with cooling breezes in distant valleys. The first time that I ever traveled through the upper reaches of the Sacramento Valley was on a rather hot and sultry day, when suddenly the temperature began to change. Cooling breezes swept in through our car and all of the passengers spoke with delight of the change in temperature. As we traveled on we soon discovered the cause of that change in the sultry temperature. We looked in the distance and saw the snow-capped peak of Mt. Shasta, towering up for more than 14,000 feet, far above all of the surrounding peaks of the mountain range. We were perhaps fifty miles away when we first noted the change in temperature. The influence of that majestic mountain affects the climate of the valleys at a distance.

The influence of the life of Jesus reaches far beyond distant valleys. It reaches through distant ages and even into the aeons of eternity. His life will never be duplicated. It will never be repeated in the same sense in which He lived as the Son of the living God. His is the one unique, sublime, majestic and over-towering life, perfect in every sense of the word, that was ever lived throughout all the ages of mankind. Christ was not only manifested in the life which He lived, but also He is manifested in the lives of those in whom He dwells and shines forth from day to day in their daily living.

Jesus was manifested in the miracles that He wrought. The wind and the waves obeyed His voice. At His command, withered limbs were made whole and the blind were made to see. Even the dead responded when He spoke and were made to live again. His voice penetrated the tomb of Lazarus after he had been dead for four days, and he was made to live again. Truly all power was given to Him in heaven and in earth. His miracles produced the greatest sensation ever manifested in any age in the world's history. The life of Jesus was the greatest of miracles as the incarnation of God. Since He Himself was the greatest miracle He was the greatest of miracle workers.

Jesus is still working miracles in the spread of His kingdom over the earth. It was more than twenty-five years ago when Miss Lela McConnell graduated from Asbury College and felt the call of God to go and invest her life in behalf of the mountaineers in eastern Kentucky. She accepted the call and began a work of faith at Mt. Carmel on the north fork of the Kentucky River in Breathitt County. She sought a hilltop on the bank of the river in a rather inaccessible place for the founding of her mountain school. No roads reached the spot. It became necessary to erect a swinging bridge across the river as an avenue of approach. The first day that she went on that hilltop with a group of friends to clear away the brush and the briars and the necessary trees, 31 blacksnakes were killed.

Today the Mt. Carmel High School enrolls approximately 100 or more students each year, and in addition to the high school, a thriving Bible Institute for training Christian workers is on another hill a mile or so away. This mountain work today has two thriving schools, a radio station, a farm, 27 outlying stations in the mountains and a staff of more than 100 workers. This work is well known as a miracle of divine grace throughout the whole of eastern Kentucky and in many parts of the nation.

The miracle-working Christ who turned the water into wine, who brought sight to blind eyes and who raised the dead is still performing mighty miracles in the earth in the spread of His kingdom over the world.

Jesus was manifested in the death that He died. He died a death which no one else ever died. The unique death of Jesus is described by the Apostle Paul in these words: "For scarcely for a righteous man will one die, yet peradventure, for a good man some would even dare to die. But God commendeth his love toward us, in that, while we were yet sinners, Christ died for us." (Romans 5:7, 8).

Christ died for sinners and not for His friends. He died for those who sought to destroy Him. Jesus knew no sin and yet He died for sinners. Paul speaks thus of His death in his letter to the Corinthians: "For he hath made him to be sin for us, who knew no sin; that we might be made the righteousness of God in him" (2 Cor. 5:21). We stand in amazement and wonder at such love that brought about such a death for sinners, and we exclaim with the Apostle John, "Behold, what man-

ner of love the Father hath bestowed upon us, that
we should be called the sons of God." Only
through the death of Jesus has it been made possible for sinners to become the sons of God.

Both God's love and justice were manifested in
regard to the sinner in the death of Jesus upon the
cross. It is an old story, often told in the older
books on theology, concerning the decree of an
ancient king. The king's decrees were like the
laws of the Medes and Persians that changeth not.
The decree went forth from the king that the pen-
alty for the violation of a certain law would de-
mand that both eyes of the person who violated
the law should be burned out with a redhot iron.
The first to violate the law was the king's own son.
His subjects stood in wonder as to what the king
might do in the case of his own son. Then they
were further amazed when the king set forth a
decree that one of his own eyes should be burned
out and likewise one eye of his son. The law was
fully satisfied when love participated in the full
measure of sacrifice in meeting the law's demands,
and it was even so that the love of God in a much
higher sense participated in a full measure of sacrifice on the cross for sinful men.

Christ was manifested in His triumphant conquest and victory over death. "Up from the grave
he arose." Death had vanquished all others, but

Christ could not be vanquished by death. He left behind an empty tomb. The keys of death and hell jangled at His girdle when He arose. His was the mightiest conquest of all the ages. All other conquests quail into insignificance beside His conquest over the grave. Because He lives, we shall live. Because He conquered, we may conquer through Him. Because He triumphed over death, we shall triumph in death. Because He abides forever, we shall abide forever. "He that doeth the will of God abideth forever." Because Christ now has a resurrected body which came triumphant out of the tomb, we shall eventually have a resurrected body "like unto his glorious body."

Christ is manifested in the victory which He gives His disciples over death. Stephen, the first Christian martyr, went from earth with a shining face amid the stones of the mob that persecuted him unto death. It was in the spring of 1938 that I had a short visit with Bishop Warren A. Candler in his home in Atlanta, Ga. Before we parted we had prayer together. When we parted, the bishop said: "One of these days you will read in the paper that I am dead. When you read it, don't believe it. It ain't so." It was a year or so later that I read on the front page of a San Francisco paper the notice of the death of Bishop Warren A. Candler. When I read it, I remembered the bishop's words,

and I said: "It ain't so." Jesus said: "I am the res-
urrection and the life: he that believeth in me,
though he were dead, yet shall he live: and who-
soever liveth and believeth in me shall never die."
(John 11:25, 26).

Christ is manifested in His disciples, whom He
sent forth into the world even as He was sent by
the Father. Jesus said in His prayer: "As thou
hast sent me into the world, even so have I also
sent them into the world." The goal and purpose
of His disciples should be, in all things, to manifest
Christ. We are His representatives in the world
and in proportion as we fail, His kingdom will fail.
The Holy Spirit manifests the name of Christ in,
and through His disciples. Men took knowledge of
the Spirit-filled Christians of the first century that
they had been with Jesus. The world still takes
knowledge of those who live in intimate fellowship with Christ.

Christ has promised that those who are sent
forth in His name shall share in His glory. Thus
He declares in His prayer: "And the glory which
thou gavest me I have given them; that they may
be one, even as we are one." Jesus gives unto His
disciples the glory of His peace and victory in a
world which is unfriendly to divine grace.

Those who are sent forth as Christ was sent
forth, shall share in His heritage. The glory of

this heritage is described by the Apostle Paul: "The spirit himself beareth witness with our spirit, that we are the children of God: and if children, then heirs; heirs of God and joint heirs with Christ; if so be that we suffer with him, that we may be also glorified together. For I reckon that the sufferings of this present time are not worthy to be compared to the glory which shall be revealed in us." (Romans 8:16-18).

Those who are sent forth as Christ was sent forth shall share with Christ in the eternal home in the city of God. The glory of that city is the glory of Christ. Jesus prayed in His prayer: "Father, I will that they also whom thou hast given me, be with me where I am; that they may behold my glory, which thou hast given me: for thou lovedst me before the foundation of the world."

Christ is making such adequate provision for those whom He has sent forth, even as He was sent forth, that there should be no worries on their part as to the future. Jesus said: "Let not your heart be troubled: ye believe in God, believe also in me. In my Father's house are many mansions, if it were not so, I would have told you. I go to prepare a place for you. If I go and prepare a place for you, I will come again, and receive you unto myself; that where I am, there ye may be also." (John 14:1-3).

CHAPTER V

There comes an increasing realization of the sublime majesty, the profound depths, and the soaring heights of Christ's valedictory prayer, each time we read it. It is beyond the reach of the finite mind to fully grasp the significance of all the statements made in the prayer. The sweep of the prayer reaches from the eternity of the past, into the eternity of the future.

The prayer was prayed under the shadow of the cross. Gethsemane and Calvary were only a few hours distant in the life of our Lord. It may be more properly designated as the Lord's prayer than the pattern prayer that was taught His disciples and which we so often repeat.

The burden of the prayer is for His disciples. The Lord gives expression to His concern for His disciples in these words: "I pray for them: I pray not for the world, but for them which thou hast given me; for they are thine. And all mine are thine, and thine are mine; and I am glorified in them." He speaks of their faith and of the experience which they had attained in Him. He commends their faith saying: "They have believed that thou didst send me.'" They had accepted

44

Christ as the true Messiah and the Saviour of the world. They had accepted Christ personally and trusted in Him for the forgiveness of their sins. In accepting Christ they had been adopted into the family of God and their names were written in the book of life. On one occasion when the disciples had been sent forth on an evangelistic tour and had returned rejoicing because the evil spirits were subject unto them, Jesus said: "Notwithstanding in this, rejoice not, that the spirits are subject unto you; but rather rejoice, because your names are written in heaven."

As followers of Christ the disciples received and believed His words with implicit confidence. Concerning their faith in His words, Jesus says: "For I have given unto them the words which thou gavest me; and they have received them, and have known surely that I came out from thee." The disciples believed the words of Jesus as completely dependable and infallible.

It is a primary and an essential step of faith to believe the Word of God if we are to obtain the blessings which are provided in His promises. God cannot honor our doubts, but He can and does honor our faith when we meet the conditions of His promises and believe His Word.

The sinner seeking the way of eternal life, will find it necessary to take an important step of faith

in connection with the promise: "But as many as
received him, to them gave he power to become
the sons of God, even to them that believe on his
name." Those who come accepting Christ should
then believe the promise that they become sons of
God.

That which God hath spoken is the anchor line
of faith that holds impregnable in every hour of
storm. Jesus met each temptation on the mount
in the bitter conflict with the adversary with the
reply, "It is written."

Christ had manifested His name unto His disciples. He says: "I have manifested thy name
unto the men which thou gavest me out of the
world." The disciples of Jesus had a definite
manifestation of God through Christ as to their
relationship with God. Christ had told them that
their names were written in heaven. They had
been assured by Christ that a mansion was being
prepared for them in the Father's house. He had
assured them that there was no necessity for worry, and that they should not let their hearts be
troubled. The manifestations given by Christ
were manifestations of assurance, comfort, and
strength.

When Jesus went away, He did not leave His
disciples without the manifestations of assurance,
comfort and strength which He gave during His

presence in the flesh. Before He went away, He promised to send another comforter who would contiuue to give these divine manifestations to His followers. Before He went away, Jesus said: "It is expedient for you that I go away, for if I go not away, the comforter will not come unto you; but if I depart, I will send him unto you."

This promise of Jesus was fulfilled and we are living today in the dispensation of the Holy Spirit. His coming on the day of Pentecost was a mighty manifestation of God's cleansing and enduing power in the lives of His disciples. Those who had been cowardly, were made bold and daring in giving their witness and testimony for Christ. Those who had been weak and vascillating, were made strong. Those who had the remains of impurity in their hearts, were made clean. Those who had been powerless, became mighty in the tearing down of the strongholds of evil. Those who had envisioned only a temporal kingdom, became enamoured with the far-flung vision of a spiritual kingdom greater in might and power than the Roman Empire.

The Holy Spirit bears witness when sinners are adopted into the family of God. Paul in his Epistle to the Romans, says: "For ye have not received the spirit of bondage again to fear; but ye have received the spirit of adoption, whereby we in connection with the promise: "But as many as received him, to them gave he power to become the sons of God, even to them that believe on his name." Those who come accepting Christ should then believe the promise that they become sons of God.

That which God hath spoken is the anchor line of faith that holds impregnable in every hour of storm. Jesus met each temptation on the mount in the bitter conflict with the adversary with the reply, "It is written."

Christ had manifested His name unto His disciples. He says: "I have manifested thy name unto the men which thou gavest me out of the world." The disciples of Jesus had a definite manifestation of God through Christ as to their relationship with God. Christ had told them that their names were written in heaven. They had been assured by Christ that a mansion was being prepared for them in the Father's house. He had assured them that there was no necessity for worry, and that they should not let their hearts be troubled. The manifestations given by Christ were manifestations of assurance, comfort, and strength.

When Jesus went away, He did not leave His disciples without the manifestations of assurance, comfort and strength which He gave during His me." He waited for some hours, until it was well up in the day. Then a flash came across the Pacific Ocean and registered in the cable office, the insignia to Bishop Candler. The bishop said: "The secret code came from our home in Atlanta from my own beloved wife, saying: 'All is well.'" That hidden secret message lifted a load from the bishop's heart. The bishop was then ready to go on a sight-seeing tour and also to travel through the country with the assurance that all was well at his Atlanta home.

It is a personal and searching question: "How is it with the home that is over there?" People ordinarily are concerned far more about the earthly house in which we dwell in this world, than about the home that is being built for them in the city of God. It is possible for us to know about that heavenly home. It is possible for those who exercise faith in Jesus Christ as Lord and Saviour, to receive an assurance, a manifestation on the part of the Holy Spirit that all is well. You may know that all is well in the heavenly home that is being prepared for you at the day of your coronation, when you shall take your departure from this world.

Christ is building for His people mansions in the eternal city. We rejoice in the blessed assurance that all is well in the city beyond the river.

Jesus said: "In my father's house are many mansions, if it were not so, I would have told you. I go to prepare a place for you. And if I go and prepare a place for you, I will come again, and receive you unto myself; that where I am there ye may be also."

Jesus commends the fact that His disciples had kept the Word of God. He said, "They have kept thy word." The word of God contains the standard for our living. It is by the Word of God that we are to direct our paths. The Psalmist said: "Thy word have I hid in mine heart that I might not sin against thee."

The disciples of Jesus rejoiced in the word of divine revelation. Jesus was faithful to the Word of God. He spoke of the Old Testament frequently and always referred to it as the Word of God. In the course of His entire ministry, Jesus never put a single question mark on the Word of God, as it had been revealed up to that time. Jesus said: "One jot nor one tittle shall in no wise pass from the law till all be fulfilled."

The disciples of Jesus were kept from evil. He says: "While I was with them in the world, I kept them in thy name." Jesus is able to keep those who commit their lives unto Him. There are those who hesitate to make a beginning in the Christian life because they are fearful that they cannot hold out. There is just one problem, and that is the problem of holding on. As long as we hold on, we are certain to hold out. Jesus has promised to keep all of those who commit their lives unto Him and place their life's destiny into His keeping.

Jesus calls attention in His prayer to the fact that His disciples were to be protected, even in their earthly life, by their faith. He said: "I pray not that thou shouldst take them out of the world, but that thou shouldest keep them from the evil." Jesus realized as He prayed that His earthly labors in the flesh were soon to be finished. He says: "I have glorified thee on the earth: I have finished the work which thou gavest me to do." He also says: "And now I am no more in the world, but these are in the world, and I come to thee. Holy Father, keep through thine own name those whom thou hast given me, that they may be one as we are."

We have a conviction that so long as we walk in the center of God's will, doing that which is pleasing in His sight, we will continue to live in this world until our work is finished. There are divine appointments relative to the termination or the continuance of our earthly labors. When Jesus prayed His valedictory prayer, the time was at hand under divine appointment for Him to complete His earthly labors. But the time was not yet at hand for His apostles to finish their labors. He prays that they might yet remain in the world and that they might be kept from the evil. There is a significant relationship to our fulfilling the will of God and being kept from evil, and to the time of our sojourn in this earthly pilgrimage.

When our lives are patterned after the will of God, we have the promise of His protecting care until our work is finished in this world. While it is true that some are taken in childhood, some in youth, some in young manhood, and some in old age, there is a divine overruling Providence in all of these departures, for those whose lives have been patterned according to His will.

The adversary could not execute his plans for the crucifixion of Jesus until His work was finished. They could not crucify Him until He had completed His mission in the world. The followers of Christ have the promise of the same divine superintendency over their lives. Jesus stated in His prayer that His disciples were sent in the same manner as He was sent. This statement of Jesus means that His disciples have the same divine superintendency as He had in relation to the sojourn of His earthly pilgrimage.

I recall the testimony of a good brother at one of my revival meetings in the town of Naylor, Mo. Brother Sands became happy as he gave his testimony. His countenance radiated joy and gladness. In the course of his testimony he said: "I am ready to go to heaven." And then after a short pause and a bit of reflection, he said: "But I don't want to go this afternoon." My reply to his statement was: "Brother Sands, God doesn't want you to go this afternoon. He is keeping you here in the world for a purpose." God in His goodness and mercy lengthens our years until our work is finished.

Jesus prayed for the sanctification of His disciples, saying: "Sanctify them through thy truth: thy word is truth." What is sanctification? Sanctification is not receiving the words of Jesus, for the disciples for whom Jesus prayed had already received His words. It is not keeping the word of God, for they had kept His Word. It is not being separated from the world, for the disciples were already a separated people. Jesus said: "They are not of the world even as I am not of the world." It is not being kept from evil, for Jesus said: "I kept them in thy name."

It is evident that the sanctification of His disciples, has a high priority with Jesus. The peroration of His prayer is for the sanctifying of His disciples.

The word "sanctify" has three major definitions in the Bible, according to Dr. Daniel Steele, the

well-known Greek scholar of the last generation
who, for some twenty years, was professor of
Greek at Boston University. One definition of
sanctification means to be set apart. It was in this
sense that the word was frequently used in the
Old Testament in relation to setting apart a building or a tabernacle for public worship.

Another meaning of sanctification relates to
those who are justified. In Paul's first epistle to
the Corinthians we find this statement: "For the
unbelieving husband is sanctified by the wife the
unbelieving wife is sanctified by the husband."
The word here has reference to salvation in the
primary sense. Sanctification begins in regeneration, in that regeneration is the first step toward
the wholly sanctified life. All who have come to a
saving knowledge of Christ are in a proper sense
candidates for entire sanctification. Those who
are justified are potentially sanctified in that they
are proper candidates for sanctification.

The word sanctify also means "to make pure,
to cleanse from moral defilement." The word is
used in this sense in a passage in Paul's Epistle to
the Ephesians: "Christ also loved the church, and
gave himself for it; that he might sanctify and
cleanse it with the washing of water by the word,
that he might present it to himself a glorious
church, not having spot, or wrinkle, or any such

thing; but that it should be holy and without blemish." (Eph. 5:25-27).

What did Christ mean when He prayed for His disciples: "Sanctify them through thy truth: thy word is truth"? As used here, the word "sanctify" does not mean to be separated and set apart, for Jesus said, "They are not of the world even as I am not of the world." They were already separated and set apart. The word in this instance cannot mean primary salvation, for the disciples were already saved, and their names were written in the book of life. It then seems clear that the word "sanctify" as Jesus uses it in this part of His petition means "to cleanse." There was yet a cleansing for the disciples of Jesus which they had not received. The need of such a cleansing was manifested in expressions of an unholy ambition on one occasion, on the part of some of His disciples. They were debating among themselves as to who would occupy the right hand, or who would occupy the left hand, when Christ came into His kingdom. All of this was displeasing to God. The Apostle John declares that the heart may be cleansed from all sin: "But if we walk in the light, as he is in the light, we have fellowship one with another, and the blood of Jesus Christ his son cleanseth us from all sin." (I John 1:7). In a still further statement, the apostle says: "If we confess our sins, he is faithful and just to forgive us our sins, and to cleanse us from all unrighteousness." (I John 1:9).

Jesus speaks of sanctifying Himself that His disciples also might be sanctified. He prays in these words: "For their sakes I sanctify myself, that they also might be sanctified through the truth." As Jesus uses the word sanctify in relation to Himself, it cannot mean cleansing, for He needed no cleansing. It cannot mean justification, for He Himself is the author of justification.

There is a relationship to the cross as Jesus uses the word sanctify concerning Himself. Jesus declares that He is setting Himself apart for the cross to be crucified for the sins of the world. He indicates that the purpose of setting Himself apart to be crucified was that His disciples also might be sanctified, or that they also might be crucified, not physically, but spiritually.

Paul knew the meaning of this personal spiritual crucifixion when he said: "I am crucified with Christ." A minister who had been praying and fasting for three days in quest of sanctification, finally went to his pulpit, and lying upon the floor beside his pulpit with his hands outstretched, prayed out of the depths of his heart: "Oh, God, drive the nails." The purifying fire of the Holy Spirit went through the preacher's heart in answer

to that earnest prayer. It was a new day in this
preacher's life. The preacher was a personal friend
of the writer. The incident which we have related
happened in a series of revival meetings in which
we were doing the preaching. That man's ministry was never the same again. He went forth in
the strength and triumph of the Pentecostal baptism until the day when the Lord sent the chariot
to take him home.

It is a searching question for each of us: "Have
the nails been driven?" Carnality resists the im-
print of the nails, but if we go all the way with our
Lord, we must bare our hearts to the searchings of
God's Holy Spirit, and face unflinchingly the inner
crucifixion of the old man of sin. Only by way of
the death route can we know the meaning of the
life "more abundantly." Jesus came not only that
we might have life, which is salvation, but also
that we might have "life more abundantly," which
is sanctification.

Christ's prayer for the sanctification of His disciples was further manifest in His prayer for their
unity in spirit: "That they all may be one; as
thou, Father, art in me, and I in thee, that they
also may be one in us." There is a vast difference
between union and unity. We have within recent
years had a significant trend toward union among
kindred groups of denominations. Such a trend is

commendable where union may be effected without the sacrifice of fundamental convictions. However, we should not mistake the union of denominational groups for that spirit of unity for which Christ prayed for His disciples. The unity of the spirit, in and through the Holy Ghost, is far greater and more important than denominational mergers. When denominational mergers are effected without the unity of the Spirit, they may prove to be of little or no value.

The goal of the sanctified life and unity of spirit in the Lord is, "That the world may believe that thou hast sent me." The day of Pentecost furnishes an example of the attainment of this goal when 3,000 persons were converted within a single day following the baptism of the 120 in the upper room with the Holy Ghost, when they were of one accord in one place, and when their hearts were purified by faith.

A further manifestation of the burden in connection with His prayer that His disciples might be sanctified is, "that they may be made perfect in one." The perfection for which Christ prayed for His disciples, is the perfection claimed by John in his first epistle in which he says: "Herein is our love made perfect, that we may have boldness in the day of judgment: because as he is, so are we in this world. There is no fear in love; but perfect love casteth out fear; because fear hath torment. He that feareth hath not been made perfect in love." (I John 4:16-18). Perfection of the head is not possible. But it is possible for the heart to be made perfect in love.

The prayer of Jesus extends far beyond the limits of this earthly sphere into the eternity that is beyond, in a divine panorama that sweeps "from glory to glory." He prays that His disciples may eventually dwell with Him in glory. He says: "Father, I will that they also, whom thou hast given me, be with me where I am; that they may behold my glory, which thou gavest me; for thou lovedst me before the foundation of the world." The glory of heaven is the glory of Christ. Heaven will be heaven because of the centrality of Christ in the eternal city. The glory of Christ will be so captivating and satisfying as to fully meet every longing and desire of the redeemed souls of earth throughout an unending eternity. Peter, James and John beheld for a short time this glory in the transfigured Christ on the mount. These apostles were so enraptured with Christ's glory in the transfiguration that they had no desire to return from the mount to the ordinary pursuits of the world. All of the redeemed of the Lord shall eventually stand in rapture in the presence of the glory of Christ, not for a brief season, as in the case of

Peter, James and John on the Mount of Transfiguration, for they shall behold His glory forever and ever. Amen.

www.ingramcontent.com/pod-product-compliance
Lightning Source LLC
Chambersburg PA
CBHW020520030426
42337CB00011B/475